HOPE
THROUGH
PROPHECY

Seven Messages to Prepare You for the Soon Return of Jesus!

Dustin Pestlin

Pacific Press®
Publishing Association
Nampa, Idaho | www.pacificpress.com

Cover design: Daniel Añez
Cover illustration: Phil McKay / www.philmckay.com
Interior design: Daniel Añez
Interior art: p. 5 © GettyImages.com, p. 7 Adobestock.com, p. 8 © GettyImages.com, p. 10 © William Brassey Hole / Goodsalt.com, p. 12 Adobestock.com, p. 13 © Prophecyart.com / Steve Creitz, p. 15 public domain, p. 16 © Prophecyart.com / Steve Creitz, p. 17 Pixabay.com, p. 19 © Pacific Press / Harry Anderson, p. 21 Adobestock.com, p. 23 © Goodsalt.com / Lars Justinen, p. 24 Prophecyart.com / Steve Creitz, p. 27 Adobestock.com, p. 28 © Goodsalt.com / Lars Justinen, p. 31 Adobestock.com, p. 35 © Goodsalt.com / Lars Justinen, p. 39 © Prophecyart.com / Steve Creitz, p. 41 © Review and Herald, p. 42 Artwork by Dustin Pestlin / images from Adobestock.com and Pixabay.com, p. 44 Adobestock.com, p. 46 Adobestock .com, p. 47 Adobestock.com, p. 48 Adobestock.com, p. 50 Pixabay.com, p. 52 Adobestock.com, p. 54 Adobestock.com, p. 56 © Goodsalt.com / Lars Justinen, p. 59 © Prophecyart.com / Steve Creitz, p. 60 Adobestock.com, p. 63 © Goodsalt.com / Phil McKay

You can obtain additional copies of this book by calling toll-free 1-800-765-6955
or by visiting http://www.adventistbookcenter.com.

ISBN 978-0-8163-6831-0

March 2022

Contents

The Authority of God's Unchangeable Word

The Bible has been burned, banned, belittled, and attacked. But it is still here. Can you trust it? How can we know that these ancient words are true?

FACT 1 **THE BIBLE IS THE BEST-SELLING BOOK IN HUMAN HISTORY**

The complete Bible has been translated into 717 languages, and the New Testament has been translated into more than 1,550 languages.[1] The Bible is also the highest-selling, most-read book in history—and no other book comes close! Guinness World Records reveals that the Bible simply dominates the all-time best-seller chart with an estimated five billion copies sold between 1815 and 2021![2]

Why is this? What makes the Bible the best-selling book in history?

According to the Bible itself, God is the true author of this best-selling book. Here is what the Bible says about itself: "All Scripture is given by inspiration of God" (2 Timothy 3:16).

FACT 2 THE BIBLE HAS SURVIVED MULTIPLE ATTACKS THROUGHOUT HISTORY

For much of recorded history, the truth of the Bible was kept in darkness.

The Bible was banned! The decree of the Council of Toulouse, made by the dominant church of the day, reads: "We prohibit also that the laity should be permitted to have the books of the Old and the New Testament; unless anyone from the motives of devotion should wish to have the Psalter or the Breviary for divine offices or the hours of the blessed Virgin; but we most strictly forbid their having any translation of these books."[3]

The Bible was publicly burned! According to the ruling of the Council of Tarragona of AD 1234: "No one may possess the books of the Old and New Testaments in the Romance language, and if anyone possesses them he must turn them over to the local bishop within eight days after the promulgation of this decree, so that they may be burned."[4]

Men and women shed their blood for the Bible that sits on your desk! John Wycliffe, who was aptly called the "Morning Star of the Reformation," was the first to translate the Bible into the English language. As a reward for this great act, he was attacked and persecuted, and even after his death his corpse "was dug up and burned. The ashes were scattered in the nearby River Swift."[5]

William Tyndale, John Huss, and many other Bible-believing Christians were killed for being champions of the Bible.

The Bible has been belittled! The story has been told of the French atheist Voltaire saying before his death, "One hundred years from today the Bible will be a forgotten book." Ironically, one hundred years after his death, Voltaire's own home was used to distribute Bibles for the French Bible Society![6] John 10:35 clearly states that "the Scripture cannot be broken."

The Bible is the most attacked book in the history of humanity, but it still stands.

FACT 3 THE BIBLE HAS BEEN PRESERVED OVER TIME

The Bible's New Testament has more than 5,800 manuscripts in the original Greek,[7] and more than 19,000 in other languages, far more than any other ancient book in the world.[8] The evidence is clear that the Bible has been uniquely preserved through the centuries.

> The words of the LORD are pure words,
> Like silver tried in a furnace of earth,
> Purified seven times.
> You shall keep them, O LORD,
> You shall preserve them from this generation forever (Psalm 12:6, 7).

The Almighty God has protected the Bible so that we can have its guidance today.

FACT 4 — SCIENCE AND ARCHAEOLOGY SUPPORT THE BIBLE

Some say that science is at odds with the Bible, but true science is always in harmony with the Bible. For example, the Bible clearly reveals the shape of the earth in Isaiah 40:22: "It is He who sits above the circle of the earth." Long before scientists knew, the Bible revealed that the earth was round.

Did you know that the Bible was the first to teach that air has weight? Job 28:25 states, "To make a weight for the wind." It took scientists until the early 1600s to make this breakthrough discovery, centuries after the Bible declared it.[9]

Archaeological finds such as the Tel Dan Stele, the Mesha Stele, the Nabonidus Cylinder, and the Dead Sea Scrolls all help prove the accuracy of the Bible.

FACT 5 — THE BIBLE HAS INTERNAL CONSISTENCY

The Bible was written over a period of 1,500 years by forty different authors. Despite many of the authors never meeting each other, they wrote with perfect internal consistency and in seamless harmony with each other's writings. Could it be that a divine hand was guiding them?

According to the Bible, this is exactly what happened: Second Peter 1:21 states that "holy men of God spoke as they were moved by the Holy Spirit."

And the sixth fact truly separates the Bible from the scriptures of every other world religion. Please read on.

FACT 6 THE BIBLE CONTAINS PROPHECY

Prophecy has been defined as history written in advance—the ability to hear from God and even predict the future with perfect accuracy. This ability is undisputable proof of divine origin.

In *Encyclopedia of Biblical Prophecy*, J. Barton Payne states that there are 1,817 prophecies in the Bible, making up about 27 percent of the Bible's total content.[10] No other world religion even comes close. And it makes sense—if someone attempts to predict the future and is wrong, that person is instantly discredited. But the Bible stands alone in its ability to accurately tell the future.

For a powerful example of an ancient Bible prophecy that came to pass exactly as the Bible predicted, check out the video titled "Daniel 2: Urgent Bible Prophecy for Today!" on the *Hope Through Prophecy* YouTube channel and read chapter 2 in this book.

As another example, let us consider the life of Jesus. There are more than 125 prophecies in the Bible's Old Testament of the coming Messiah, the One who would die for the sins of humanity. Jesus perfectly fulfilled each and every one of these Old Testament prophecies! Dr. Peter Stoner, a mathematician and former chairman at Pasadena City College, calculated that the odds of one man fulfilling just 8 of these 125-plus prophecies is one in ten to the thirty-third power![11]

God knows the end from the beginning. This separates the God of the Bible from all other gods. Isaiah 46:9, 10, declares, "I am God, and there is none like Me, declaring the end from the beginning, and from ancient times things that are not yet done."

But perhaps the most powerful evidence for the authority of the Bible is this seventh undeniable fact.

FACT 7 THE BIBLE CHANGES LIVES

The Bible states: "Therefore, if anyone is in Christ, he is a new creation; old things have passed away; behold, all things have become new" (2 Corinthians 5:17).

I have seen countless lives transformed by the powerful message of the Bible. It makes the drunkard sober, it makes the hateful kind, it shows how we can attain victory over our bad habits and how we can receive eternal life.

In my case, the teachings of the Bible have given purpose and direction to my life and hope for the future. I know that it can do the same for you.

It will help you answer life's three most important questions: *Where did I come from? Why am I here? Where am I going?*

Dear friends, I commend to you the Bible: the inspired Word of God. This book has been tested by time and has been proven trustworthy. It is a book that stands apart from the rest. It is a book that you can build your life on.

In these pages, and on my YouTube channel, you have my commitment to let the Bible—*and only the Bible*—be the standard, the benchmark, and the final authority.

When it comes to vital truth, if it is in the Bible, I want it. If it is not in the Bible, it is not for me. I appeal to each of you to let the Bible be the guide for your life. If this is your desire, ask God to send the Holy Spirit so you can understand it. Read it every day, and be willing to follow its teachings.

The video for this chapter is on YouTube. Search for "Seven Incredible Bible Facts That Will Blow Your Mind," or scan this QR code.

1. "Our Impact," Wycliffe Bible Translators, accessed February 10, 2022, wycliffe.org.uk/about/our-impact/.

2. "Best-Selling Book," Guiness World Records, accessed February 10, 2021, https://www.guinnessworldrecords.com/world-records/best-selling-book-of-non-fiction.

3. "The Council of Toulouse, 1229," in *Heresy and Authority in Medieval Europe*, ed. Edward Peters (Philadelphia: University of Pennsylvania Press, 1980), 195, quoted in "The Bible Forbidden to the Laity," Just for Catholics, accessed February 10, 2022, http://www.justforcatholics.org/a198.htm.

4. D. Lortsch, *Histoire de la Bible en France* (1910), 14, quoted in "Why Do You Accuse the Catholic Church of Being Against the Bible?" BibleAsk, accessed March 11, 2022, https://bibleask.org/why-do-you-accuse-the-catholic-church-of-being-against-the-bible/.

5. Richard Cavendish, "John Wycliffe Condemned as a Heretic," *History Today*, May 2015, https://www.historytoday.com/archive/john-wycliffe-condemned-heretic.

6. John Pritchard, "Bible Sunday," Bible Society, accessed March 11, 2022, https://www.biblesociety.org.uk/content/get_involved/bible_sunday/2016_resources/Bible-Sunday-Sermon-notes.pdf.

7. Bryan Windle, "The Earliest New Testament Manuscripts," Bible Archaeology Report, February 15, 2019, https://biblearchaeologyreport.com/2019/02/15/the-earliest-new-testament-manuscripts/.

8. Edward Antonio, "Why Are There So Many Different Versions of the Bible?" Christianity.com, July 15, 2019, https://www.christianity.com/wiki/bible/why-are-there-so-many-different-versions-of-the-bible.html.

9. "Everest," Nova Online Adventure, PBS.org, accessed March 28, 2022, https://www.pbs.org/wgbh/nova/everest/earth/air.html

10. J. Barton Payne, *Encyclopedia of Biblical Prophecy* (Eugene, OR: Wipf and Stock, 2020; New York: Harper and Row, 1973), 13, 675.

11. "Is Jesus for Real? Can There Actually Be Mathematical Proof?" Jesus: Fraud or Messiah?, BibleTimelines.com, accessed February 10, 2022, https://www.bibletimelines.net/articles/is-jesus-really-the-messiah.

Portions of this book have been adapted with permission from Amazing Facts Bible Study Guides and Mark Finley, *Studying Together*. "Bible Study Guides—English," Amazing Facts.org, accessed March 28, 2022, https://www.amazingfacts.org/media-library/read/c/2/t/bible-study-guides. Mark Finley, *Studying Together* (N.P.: Hart Research, 1995).

Much of this chapter has been adapted with permission from Dwight Nelson. Dwight Nelson,"War," Dwight Nelson: Rumors From the East, AudioVerse.org, accessed March 28, 2022, https://www.audioverse.org/en/teachings/558/war.html

Daniel 2: Ancient Bible Prophecy for Today

Is it possible that a prophecy written twenty-five hundred years ago has something to say about world history and our current situation?

The Old Testament book of Daniel was written in the sixth century BC. Skeptics have tried to discredit this book by placing the date of its writing at a later time, but archaeological evidence such as the dating of the Dead Sea Scrolls help show that Daniel was indeed written during the time the Bible claims it was.

As we turn to the second chapter of this prophetic book, we find ourselves in the courts of ancient Babylon. The great king Nebuchadnezzar has invaded Judah and taken Daniel and his friends captive with the intention of educating them in the Babylonian system of government.

The chapter begins with the king being troubled by a startling nightmare. He calls for the best and brightest men of His kingdom to reveal to the king both his dream and its interpretation.

These pagan men accurately declare to the king: "There is not a man on earth who can tell the king's matter; . . . It is a difficult thing that the king requests, and there is no other who can tell it to the king except the gods" (Daniel 2:10, 11).

These men know that only a divine power can reveal the kind of information the king is demanding. In his fury, the king then announces that all the wise men of Babylon should be killed.

The message soon comes to Daniel and his friends, Hebrews who worship the God of the Bible. Rather than panic, Daniel calmly requests some time, so that he can join his friends in prayer to seek an understanding of the king's vision.

His prayer is recorded in Daniel 2:20–23:

> Blessed be the name of God forever and ever,
> For wisdom and might are His.
> And He changes the times and the seasons;
> He removes kings and raises up kings;
> He gives wisdom to the wise
> And knowledge to those who have understanding.
> He reveals deep and secret things;
> He knows what is in the darkness,
> And light dwells with Him.
>
> I thank You and praise You,
> O God of my fathers;
> You have given me wisdom and might,
> And have now made known to me what we asked of You,
> For You have made known to us the king's demand.

God has revealed the king's dream to Daniel!

Daniel is then quickly rushed into the king's presence. Nebuchadnezzar eagerly asks Daniel if he is able to reveal the dream to him, and Daniel responds with great wisdom: "The secret which the king has demanded, the wise men, the astrologers, the magicians, and the sooth-sayers cannot declare to the king. But there is a God in heaven who reveals secrets, and He has made known to King Nebuchadnezzar what will be in the latter days" (verses 27, 28).

Here Daniel is giving all the credit to God. He is also showing the difference between the true God of the Bible and all the other false religions that claim to know the truth.

Daniel now reveals the dream:

> You, O king, were watching; and behold, a great image! This great image, whose splendor was excellent, stood before you; and its form was awesome. This image's head was of fine gold, its chest and arms of silver, its belly and thighs of bronze, its legs of iron, its feet partly of iron and partly of clay. You watched while a stone was cut out without hands, which struck the image on its feet of iron and clay, and broke them in pieces. Then the iron, the clay, the bronze, the silver, and the gold were crushed together, and became like chaff from the summer threshing floors; the wind

carried them away so that no trace of them was found. And the stone that struck the image became a great mountain and filled the whole earth (verses 31–35).

By now the king is most certainly on the edge of his seat, hanging on Daniel's every word! Daniel then confidently proceeds to reveal the meaning of the dream to the king.

"You, O king, are a king of kings. For the God of heaven has given you a kingdom, power, strength, and glory; . . . you are this head of gold" (verses 37, 38).

Daniel clearly identifies King Nebuchadnezzar and his mighty kingdom of Babylon as the head of gold represented in this dream.

Gold was a fitting symbol for Babylon. Its wealth and greatness were unrivaled in the ancient world.

Greek historian Herodotus notes that "Babylon surpasses in splendor any city in the known world." He goes on to describe the outer walls of Babylon to be 320 feet high, 56 miles long, and 80 feet thick—wide enough to race multiple chariots side by side on top of them.[1]

Babylon could also boast of its famous hanging gardens—one of the seven wonders of the ancient world. However, much to the king's dismay, his kingdom would not last forever.

Daniel 2:39 reads, "But after you shall arise another kingdom inferior to yours."

The history books certainly confirm this. Babylon was overtaken. The Medo-Persian Empire would become the next world power. And before Media-Persia came to rule, the Bible identified this kingdom by name. Daniel 8:20 specifically refers to "the kings of Media and Persia" in a repeated version of the same prophecy.

The Persian army, led by Cyrus the Great, conquered Babylon in 539 BC. Silver was a fitting metal to represent this kingdom, as Media-Persia was inferior to Babylon and used silver as a primary mode of currency.

Daniel continues to boldly reveal the dream's meaning by describing the third metal: "A third kingdom of bronze, which shall rule over all the earth" (Daniel 2:39).

Historians agree that this next kingdom, led by Alexander the Great, was none other than the kingdom of Greece.

The Bible, once again, accurately predicted the arrival of this kingdom by name, centuries before it rose to power. Daniel 8:21 mentions "the kingdom of Greece" as being the kingdom that would conquer Media-Persia.

Daniel next addresses the legs of iron: "And the fourth kingdom shall be as strong as iron, inasmuch as iron breaks in pieces and shatters everything; and like iron that crushes, that kingdom will break in pieces and crush all the others" (Daniel 2:40).

A more fitting description could not be given for the fourth kingdom—the powerful Roman Empire. Known for its dominant army and brutal power, Rome has been given the fitting nickname the Iron Monarchy.

This empire, mentioned in both the Old and the New Testaments of the Bible, ruled during the time of Christ. Roman soldiers whipped Jesus with an iron cat-o'-nine-tails, drove iron nails into His innocent hands, and pierced His side with an iron spear.

So far God has revealed the rise and fall of four powerful world empires. The history books confirm the accuracy of this amazing prophecy.

But Daniel is not finished. He goes on to describe the feet of this great image, and with incredible detail reveals their historical significance:

> Whereas you saw the feet and toes, partly of potter's clay and partly of iron, the kingdom shall be divided; yet the strength of the iron shall be in it, just as you saw the iron mixed with ceramic clay. And as the toes of the feet were partly of iron and

partly of clay, so the kingdom shall be partly strong and partly fragile. As you saw iron mixed with ceramic clay, they will mingle with the seed of men; but they will not adhere to one another, just as iron does not mix with clay (verses 41–43).

History affirms the Bible's account that Rome was not overtaken by a single dominant empire but was divided up into several nations. These nations are what we know today as modern Europe.

Amazingly, Daniel reveals that these nations would not "adhere to one another" (verse 43); that is, they would never unite into one dominant kingdom. Incredibly, history reveals that even this very detailed part of the prophecy is accurate.

Daniel mentions that they would "mingle with the seed of men" (verse 43). This was clearly fulfilled by the frequent intermarriage of European royalty throughout the centuries. But, as the Bible predicted, these nations would not unite in any significant fashion.

Charlemagne tried to unite Europe and failed. Napoleon tried to unite Europe and failed. Hitler, despite controlling the majority of the continent at one point and being poised to take control of the Western world, failed to unite Europe.

Europe has never been and never will be united into one empire. The Bible's predictions have always come to pass, and they will never fail. This prophecy of Daniel has revealed twenty-five hundred years of Earth's history with striking, pinpoint accuracy.

But friends, there is still one part of the prophecy of Daniel 2 that is yet to be fulfilled. And we can be certain that it will come to pass just as surely as the rest of the prophecy.

Speaking of the days of modern Europe, in which we live today, Daniel exclaims: "And in the days of these kings the God of heaven will set up a kingdom which shall never be destroyed; and the kingdom shall not be left to other people; it shall break in pieces and consume all these kingdoms, and it shall stand forever" (verse 44).

Daniel clearly states the final event of this groundbreaking prophecy. The God of heaven will set up a kingdom that will never be destroyed.

Dear reader, you can be a part of this kingdom! You can live forever in Paradise with the God of the universe! I would like to support you as you prepare for this great adventure and show you from the Bible how you can be a part of it.

If you would like to learn more about the Bible's teachings, and how they apply to your life, I encourage you to continue reading this book, to watch the *Hope Through Prophecy* YouTube channel, and to start a practice of consistent Bible study and prayer.

The video for this chapter is on YouTube. Search for "Daniel 2: Urgent Bible Prophecy for Today (2020)," or scan this QR code.

1. John Gaston, "The Seven Wonders of the World," SermonCentral, November 27, 2016, https://www.sermoncentral.com/sermons/the-seven-wonders-of-the-world-john-gaston-sermon-on-jesus-sacrifice-205392?page=1&wc=800.

What Must I Do to Be Saved?

What exactly must I do to be saved, forgiven, and receive eternal life?
What does the ancient sanctuary service teach us about God's plan of
salvation? Let's reflect on the answers to these questions and more.

To understand salvation, we need to study the story of salvation

The story of salvation shows how we can have peace with God and live with Him forever. We begin in the Garden of Eden, a paradise that God created for humanity. We read in Genesis 2:15, "Then the LORD God took the man and put him in the garden of Eden to tend and keep it."

This garden was pure and beautiful, and humanity was created to live on this Earth forever, with no death, sin, or suffering. Adam and Eve, the original humans, were directed to "be fruitful and multiply; fill the earth and subdue it" (Genesis 1:28).

But God gave this first couple a single rule to test their allegiance to Him and prove that they were worthy of this wonderful gift of life.

"And the LORD God commanded the man, saying, 'Of every tree of the garden you may freely eat; but of the tree of the knowledge of good and evil you shall not eat, for in the day that you eat of it you shall surely die.' " (Genesis 2:16, 17).

Unfaithful to God's trust, the first couple broke His plain command and ate of the forbidden fruit. We read of this sad account in Genesis 3:6, which says, "So when the woman saw that the tree was good for food, that it was pleasant to the eyes, and a tree desirable to make one wise, she took of its fruit and ate. She also gave to her husband with her, and he ate."

So what would be the result?

The Bible is direct in describing the results of sin. Romans 6:23 says: "For the wages of sin is death."

In fact, we have seen that God clearly said, "In the day that you eat of it you shall surely die" (Genesis 2:17).

All of the universe was watching this scene with great interest. The fate of humanity was hanging in the balance. What would happen next? Would the death sentence be carried out, or would Adam and Eve, and all of humanity, be given a second chance?

Friends, humanity needed a hero that day. Someone had to step in to provide a way out. We needed Someone who would die in our place so that we might live.

We read of this sacrifice in the book of Revelation, where it refers to the "Lamb slain from the foundation of the world" (Revelation 13:8).

In the courts of heaven above, as the fate of humanity was discussed, a voice rang out exclaiming: "I will pay the price! I will die the death that they deserve, so that they can live the life that I deserve. The human race will have a second chance!"

The universe listened in silence and awe.

Could it be? Jesus Christ, the God of the universe, sacrificing His own life for wicked human beings?

Yes, this Lamb is Jesus!

Jesus fulfilled Bible prophecy!

He is the Lamb of Revelation!

In the Old Testament of the Bible, there are more than 190 prophetic references to the coming Messiah, the Lamb of God.[1] Jesus fulfilled each of them perfectly.

We read about Him in John 1:29: "The next day John saw Jesus coming toward him, and said, 'Behold! The Lamb of God who takes away the sin of the world!' "

We learn about salvation from the sanctuary in Bible times

To better understand this, let us turn our attention to the sanctuary service of ancient Israel. After all, God tells us that His way, His plan of salvation, can be seen in the sanctuary.

The Bible declares: "Your way, O God, is in the sanctuary; who is so great a God as our God?" (Psalm 77:13).

The sanctuary was a three-dimensional blueprint, or model, of God's true sanctuary in heaven. It was given to God's people to teach them more about His character and His plan to save humanity. The building plans for this awe-inspiring structure were given to Moses on Mount Sinai.

In the sanctuary, when an Israelite sinned, they were required to bring a perfect, spotless lamb into the court of the sanctuary. They had to lay their hands on its head, symbolizing the transfer of sin from the person to the innocent lamb.

What happened next was graphic and sad but was meant to show the pain and suffering that sin causes. The sinner, with his own hands, was to slit the throat of the blameless lamb, spilling its blood (see Leviticus 1:1, 2, 4, 11). The Bible teaches that without the shedding of blood there is no forgiveness of sins (Hebrews 9:22).

Consider the connection to the following words: "In Him [Jesus] we have redemption through His blood, the forgiveness of sins, according to the riches of His grace" (Ephesians 1:7).

By participating in this ceremony, the sinner was forgiven as he showed his faith in the true Lamb of God, the Messiah, who was to come. Just as the lambs in the sanctuary service had to be perfect and spotless, Jesus was without sin, fully innocent.

The lamb symbolically took on the sins of the people and paid their penalty. This represented the fact that Jesus took the blame for the sins of the entire world, and He paid the ultimate penalty, which was death.

The death of Jesus opened the door to our salvation

You have probably heard this beautiful verse: "For God so loved the world that He gave His only begotten Son, that whoever believes in Him should not perish but have everlasting life" (John 3:16).

The God of the universe humbled Himself and became a human being. He lived a life of sacrifice and loving service. He suffered and bled and died on the cross to take the death penalty that you and I deserve. What wonderful love is this! But that is not the end of the story. Because of Jesus' victory over sin, death could not hold Him down. After three days in the tomb, Jesus rose up victorious!

As angels stood by the door of the empty tomb, they exclaimed, "He is not here; for He is risen, as He said. Come, see the place where the Lord lay" (Matthew 28:6).

By conquering death, Jesus has opened the door for us to live with Him forever!

So what exactly must we do to receive the free gift of salvation that Jesus paid for on the cross? I will explain this in just a moment.

Jesus' death and resurrection can change our lives

But first, what does Jesus' death and resurrection mean to you? How do they affect your life?

1. No matter how evil you may be, all your past sins will be forgiven. "If we confess our sins, He is faithful and just to forgive us our sins and to cleanse us from all unrighteousness" (1 John 1:9).

2. You become adopted into the family of God. "But as many as received Him, to them He gave the right to become children of God, to those who believe in His name" (John 1:12).

3. You will live a more joyful, abundant life. "I have come that they may have life, and that they may have it more abundantly" (John 10:10). We now have a purpose for our life and a hope for the future. No matter what struggles come our way—if we lose property, health, or even life—we know that Jesus is at our side and will never leave us. We know that we have eternal life secured. What peace and joy this will bring you!

4. He changes your heart and attitude. "Therefore, if anyone is in Christ, he is a new creation; old things have passed away; behold,

all things have become new" (2 Corinthians 5:17). He helps us abandon the sinful things we used to do. The drunkard becomes sober. The angry person becomes patient and kind. Jesus gives us power to live holy lives! This will strengthen your marriage, improve your relationships with your children and friends, and positively impact all areas of your life.

5. If you are faithful to Him, you will live with Jesus forever on the new earth. Jesus tells us: "In My Father's house are many mansions. . . . I go to prepare a place for you" (John 14:2).

So how can you make these things a reality? How can you secure these blessings for yourself? What must you do to be saved?

Friend, the forgiveness and abundant life that Jesus offers can be yours in this very moment. Please do not take this decision lightly—it will be the most important of your life. By choosing Jesus as your Lord and Savior, you are choosing to say goodbye to a life of sin and death, and you are accepting a life of love, joy, and obedience.

I want to give you this opportunity to accept Jesus as your Lord and Savior right now or to rededicate yourself to Him at this time. If this is your desire, I invite you to say this prayer with me:

> Dear Lord, I know that I am a sinner worthy of death.
> There is nothing I can do to save myself from the punishment of death.
> I believe that You died for me on the cross to pay the penalty for my sins so that I can have eternal life.
> Thank You for making this sacrifice for me.
> Please forgive my past sins. I turn from them now.
> I choose to surrender my life to You and to accept You as my Lord and Savior.
> Help me live a holy life that honors You.
> I pray this prayer in Jesus' name. Amen.

Dear reader, you have just made the greatest decision of your life. Now stay close to Jesus!

If you have made this decision for the first time, or if you would like to affirm your commitment to follow Jesus, I encourage you to say out loud, "Jesus, I'm Yours."

In the following chapters, I will share more about how to maintain and strengthen this life-changing decision. You will learn groundbreaking information that will help prepare you for the return of our Savior. And always, keep your eyes on Jesus, the Author and Finisher of your faith!

The video for this chapter is on YouTube. Search for "Salvation: How to Have Eternal Life (Life-Changing)," or scan this QR code.

1. J. Barton Payne, *Encyclopedia of Biblical Prophecy* (Eugene, OR: Wipf and Stock, 2020; New York: Harper and Row, 1973), 675.

Ten Facts About the Soon Return of Jesus

The second coming of Jesus Christ is the most anticipated event in human history, and it is soon to come. However, millions have been deceived on this topic.

The return of Jesus to Earth is the blessed hope for all Christians. It captivates the imagination and warms the heart. However, many sincere Christians have dangerous misunderstandings about this great event that could cost them their eternal life. Here are ten facts from the Bible about the return of Jesus, so that you can be ready for it.

1. When Jesus returns, every eye will see Him

Yes, the second coming of Jesus will be fully visible!

"Behold, He is coming with clouds, and every eye will see Him, even they who pierced Him.

And all the tribes of the earth will mourn because of Him. Even so, Amen" (Revelation 1:7).

Notice that *every* eye will witness this great event.

In fact, the Bible compares the return of Jesus to an explosive blast of lightning, bursting across the sky: "For as the lightning comes from the east and flashes to the west, so also will the coming of the Son of Man be" (Matthew 24:27).

2. When Jesus returns, every ear will hear Him

The return of Christ will be fully *audible*: "For the Lord Himself will descend from heaven with a shout, with the voice of an archangel, and with the trumpet of God. And the dead in Christ will rise first" (1 Thessalonians 4:16).

Yes, the very trumpet of God will echo through the sky like claps of roaring thunder, so powerful that it will even wake the dead!

3. When Jesus returns, all His angels will be with Him

At His first coming, Jesus came as a humble baby, but when He returns, it will be as conquering King, and all His mighty army will be with Him.

"When the Son of Man comes in His glory, and all the holy angels with Him, then He will sit on the throne of His glory" (Matthew 25:31).

Friends, Jesus will not return alone. He will be accompanied by all of the armies of heaven, a mighty multitude of holy angels.

4. When Jesus returns, there will be a great earthquake

Upon the return of Jesus, the greatest earthquake in human history will rock this earth to its very core: "And there were noises and thunderings and lightnings; and there was a great earthquake, such a mighty and great earthquake as had not occurred since men were on the earth" (Revelation 16:18).

In fact, the Bible says that this quake will be so powerful that even mountains and islands will disappear, and the cities of the earth will be devastated (Revelation 6:12–14).

5. When Jesus returns, He will have a real body

Some people believe that Jesus will come back as a spiritual being, not possessing an actual human body. Is this true? Let us consider what the angels said when Jesus left this earth at His first coming: "Now when He had spoken these things, while they watched, He was taken up, and a cloud received Him out of their sight. And while they looked steadfastly toward heaven as He went up, behold, two men stood by them in white apparel, who also said, 'Men of Galilee, why do you stand gazing up into heaven? This same Jesus, who was taken up from you into heaven, will so come in like manner as you saw Him go into heaven' " (Acts 1:9–11).

Notice that the angels said that Jesus will return in *like manner* as He left. When He left this earth, Jesus had a real physical body. We know this because, after He was resurrected, Jesus told His disciples the following: "Behold My hands and My feet, that it is I Myself. Handle and see, for a spirit does not have flesh and bones as you see I have" (Luke 24:39).

Jesus will return with this same physical body.

There is a popular teaching in the Christian world today known as the secret rapture. The

Bible says nothing about such a thing. In fact, so far, we have seen that Jesus' return will be visible, audible, global, physical, and will be accompanied by a worldwide, devastating earthquake. There is nothing secret about this majestic event.

6. When Jesus Returns, He will come with a reward for each person

"And behold, I am coming quickly, and My reward is with Me, to give to every one according to his work" (Revelation 22:12).

This verse shows us that Jesus will have already judged and determined the fate of every human being prior to His return. After all, He is bringing His reward with Him.

God's final warning to the world in the book of Revelation, known as the three angels' messages (Revelation 14:6–12), reveals that the judgment takes place in the end time, *before* the return of Jesus: "Then I saw another angel flying in the midst of heaven, having the everlasting gospel to preach to those who dwell on the earth—to every nation, tribe, tongue, and people—saying with a loud voice, 'Fear God and give glory to Him, for the hour of His judgment has come; and worship Him who made heaven and earth, the sea and springs of water' " (Revelation 14:6, 7).

My friend, God's judgment is taking place right now! For more information about the judgment and to learn how you can stand victorious, watch the video "God's End-Time Judgment" on the *Hope Through Prophecy* YouTube channel.

7. When Jesus returns, the wicked will be destroyed

The popular secret rapture theory teaches that the evil people will be left alive after the second coming of Jesus; but friends, nothing could be further from the truth. The Bible says, "And at that day the slain of the Lord shall be from one end of the earth even to the other end of the earth. They shall not be lamented, or gathered, or buried; they shall become refuse on the ground" (Jeremiah 25:33).

A verse that is often used to support the secret rapture is Luke 17:36: "Two men will be in the field: the one will be taken and the other left." However, this passage of Luke 17:26–37 is comparing the destruction of Sodom and Noah's flood with the time of the second coming of Christ. It is saying that in both of these cases, the righteous were saved, and the wicked were destroyed. Speaking of the wicked, Jesus says in verse 37, "Wherever the body is, there the eagles will be gathered together." This same scene of the birds feasting on the flesh of the wicked is described in Revelation 18:7, 8. In Luke 17, Jesus is making it clear that the wicked will be destroyed when He returns, which is in harmony with the rest of Scripture.

8. When Jesus returns, the righteous who are dead will be resurrected

But those who have been faithful to God and have accepted Jesus as their Savior and Lord will come out from the grave at the sound of His mighty voice. They have learned to love that voice, and now they will meet their blessed Savior face-to-face. I can imagine family members reuniting on that day, tears streaming down their faces as they look up toward their loving King.

"For the Lord Himself will descend from heaven with a shout, with the voice of an archangel, and with the trumpet of God. And the dead in Christ will rise first" (1 Thessalonians 4:16).

9. When Jesus returns, the righteous who are alive will meet Him in the air

The righteous who are living when Christ returns will witness this spectacular event: "Then we who are alive and remain shall be caught up together with them in the clouds to meet the Lord in the air. And thus we shall always be with the Lord" (1 Thessalonians 4:17).

You will notice that the righteous will meet the Lord *in the air*. Jesus will not touch the ground at His second coming. This is a crucial point that will help you avoid being deceived. The Bible speaks of false Christs in the last days and warns us not to go after them: "And they will say to you, 'Look here!' or 'Look there!' Do not go after them or follow them" (Luke 17:23).

10. When Jesus returns, many will be unprepared

As we look at the world around us, the signs of the times are being fulfilled before our very eyes. Scripture warns that these things would happen and tells us to be ready when they do.

These things have been happening since the beginning of time, but never with the *intensity* and *frequency* that they are happening today. This world can be compared to a pregnant woman, whose labor pains are becoming more intense and frequent, signaling that she is soon to give birth.

The Bible also describes those who mock the idea that Jesus is coming soon: "Knowing this first: that scoffers will come in the last days, walking according to their own lusts, and saying, 'Where is the promise of His coming? For since the fathers fell asleep, all things continue as they were from the beginning of creation' " (2 Peter 3:3, 4).

For those who do not prepare for it, Jesus' return will come unexpectedly: "For you yourselves know perfectly that the day of the Lord so comes as a thief in the night" (1 Thessalonians 5:2).

This does not mean that Jesus' return will be a secret; instead, it means that many will be unprepared for it. Jesus warns us to be ready at all times for His return: "Therefore you also be ready, for the Son of Man is coming at an hour you do not expect" (Matthew 24:44).

We can be 100 percent certain that Jesus is coming again—and He has prepared a place just for you in His heavenly kingdom: "In My Father's house are many mansions; if it were not so, I would have told you. I go to prepare a place for you" (John 14:2).

But dear friend, sin cannot exist in the presence of a holy God. When Jesus returns, He will destroy sin, and anyone who chooses to cling to it.

Let us give our lives to Him today, so that He can forgive our sins and give us the power to a live a victorious life, preparing for His soon return.

Jesus is inviting you today to allow Him into your life: "Behold, I stand at the door and knock. If anyone hears My voice and opens the door, I will come in to him and dine with him, and he with Me" (Revelation 3:20).

Will you let Him in? If it is your desire to choose Jesus as your Lord and Savior and to be ready for His soon return, just say out loud, "Lord, I choose You today."

Amen!

If you would like to enroll in a free Bible study course or would like to find a church that teaches the Bible truths shared in this booklet, email us at bible@hopethroughprophecy.org. This material is adapted from video presentations on a YouTube channel named *Hope Through Prophecy*. If you haven't already done so, please search for *Hope Through Prophecy* on YouTube, or feel free to scan the code below on your smartphone. Remember, friend, keep your eyes on Jesus, the Author and Finisher of our faith!

The video for this chapter is on YouTube. Search for "10 Things That Will Happen When Jesus Returns," or scan this QR code.

The Antichrist: Ten Proofs From the Bible

This mysterious entity is at the center of end-time Bible prophecy and will even be responsible for the infamous mark of the beast. Fortunately, thanks to the Bible, there is no need to guess the identity of this diabolical power.

The antichrist. The very word has been the source of fascination and intrigue for thousands of years. Numerous theories have been proposed about who the antichrist truly is. In this chapter, we will provide no speculation or rumors but will go right to the Bible to identify this antichrist power.

Referring to the apocalyptic book of Revelation, the Bible says, "The Revelation of Jesus Christ, which God gave Him to show His servants—things which must shortly take place. And

He sent and signified it by His angel to His servant John. . . . Blessed is he who reads and those who hear the words of this prophecy, and keep those things which are written in it; for the time is near" (Revelation 1:1, 3).

You will notice that the book of Revelation is about Jesus and from Him, and a blessing is pronounced on those who listen to and obey its words. Therefore, although the message about the antichrist is a solemn warning, it is part of the revelation of Jesus Christ and comes from His heart of love. He wants us to know the truth so we can be protected and saved.

Revelation 14 contains the three angels' messages: God's final warning to the world. The third angel specifically warns about the beast, another name for the antichrist, and its mark: "Then a third angel followed them, saying with a loud voice, 'If anyone worships the beast and his image, and receives his mark on his forehead or on his hand, he himself shall also drink of the wine of the wrath of God, which is poured out full strength into the cup of His indignation' " (verses 9, 10). The greatest judgments in human history are prepared for those who worship this antichrist beast and receive its mark.

Bible prophecy sometimes refers to entities known as beasts. What does the Bible mean? The book of Revelation is full of symbolism. In order for us to identify the meaning of the symbols,

we must let the Bible interpret itself. So according to the Bible, what does a beast represent?

The book of Daniel uses the term *beast* several times (Daniel 7:3, 5–7, 17, 19). Now notice Daniel 7:23: "The fourth beast shall be a fourth kingdom on earth."

The Bible is revealing to us that a beast represents a kingdom in apocalyptic prophecy.

Now brace yourselves, friends. This mysterious beast, or kingdom, that will enforce the mark of the beast is vividly described in Revelation 13: "Then I stood on the sand of the sea. And I saw a beast rising up out of the sea, having seven heads and ten horns, and on his horns ten crowns, and on his heads a blasphemous name" (verse 1).

We will now consider this beast of Revelation 13 and ten characteristics that describe it in detail before we positively identify this antichrist power. God provides multiple characteristics of the beast because He wants us to have no doubt about its identity.

As we consider these ten characteristics, ask yourself who this power is. Students of history will most likely recognize it before it is revealed later in this chapter.

1. The beast rises out of the sea

"Then I stood on the sand of the sea. And I saw a beast rising up out of the sea" (Revelation 13:1). According to the Bible, a sea represents a heavily populated area: "The waters which you saw . . . are peoples, multitudes, nations, and tongues" (Revelation 17:15). Therefore, we conclude that this beast, or kingdom, arises from a heavily populated area.

2. The best receives its throne, power, and authority from the dragon

"The dragon gave him his power, his throne, and great authority" (Revelation 13:2). This beast receives its power and authority from the dragon. Who or what is the dragon? We know from the Bible that the dragon represents Satan. However, the Bible is actually more specific about who this dragon is: "And another sign appeared in heaven: behold, a great, fiery red dragon having seven heads and ten horns, and seven diadems on his heads. His tail drew a third of the stars of heaven and threw them to the earth. And the dragon stood before the woman who was ready to give birth, to devour her Child as soon as it was born. She bore a male Child who was to rule all nations with a rod of iron. And her Child was caught up to God and His throne" (Revelation 12:3–5). This passage refers to the birth of Christ and how Satan tried to destroy Christ at His birth. Which power did Satan work through to try to accomplish this? It was Rome. Herod, a leader in the pagan Roman Empire, tried to destroy Jesus at His birth. So according to Revelation, Rome is directly connected to the dragon's power, throne, and authority.

Some of you may be starting to see which historical power matches these descriptions.

3. The beast is a global power

"And I saw one of his heads as if it had been mortally wounded, and his deadly wound was healed. And all the world marveled and followed the beast. . . .

. . . And authority was given him over every tribe, tongue, and nation" (Revelation 13:3, 7).

Clearly, the antichrist has global power and influence.

4. The beast is guilty of blasphemy

"I saw a beast rising up out of the sea, having seven heads and ten horns, and on his horns ten crowns, and on his heads a blasphemous name. . . .

. . .Then he opened his mouth in blasphemy against God, to blaspheme His name, His tabernacle, and those who dwell in heaven" (Revelation 13:1, 6).

The Bible describes blasphemy in two ways:

1. **You commit blasphemy when you claim the power to forgive sins (Luke 5:21).**
2. **You commit blasphemy when you claim to be God Himself (John 10:33).**

This beast power is guilty of both forms of blasphemy. Which organization could this be referring to? We will soon find out.

5. The beast ruled during forty-two prophetic months

"And he was given a mouth speaking great things and blasphemies, and he was given authority to continue for forty-two months" (Revelation 13:5). In Bible prophecy, one prophetic day equals one literal year. We see this principle in Numbers 14:34 and Ezekiel 4:6, which reads, "I have laid on you a day for each year."

So this antichrist power ruled for forty-two prophetic months. This amounts to 1,260 days in the Hebrew calendar, and, according to the day-year principle in Ezekiel, it refers to 1,260 literal years. Interestingly, this 1,260-year reign for the antichrist is referenced seven times in the prophetic books of Daniel and Revelation!

6. The beast received a deadly wound that later healed

"And I saw one of his heads as if it had been mortally wounded, and his deadly wound was healed. And all the world marveled and followed the beast" (Revelation 13:3). The Bible speaks of this beast power receiving a deadly wound, which would later be healed. We will shortly reveal how this very thing happened to the antichrist.

7. The beast receives worship

"They worshiped the beast, saying, 'Who is like the beast? Who is able to make war with him?' " (Revelation 13:4). Clearly, this beast power differs from other nations due to the fact that it receives worship. This indicates that the antichrist is both a political and religious power.

8. The beast persecutes God's people

"It was granted to him to make war with the saints and to overcome them" (Revelation 13:7). The antichrist is guilty of making war against God's very own people. Later in this chapter, we will pull back the curtain on this blasphemous opponent of God and His saints.

9. The beast has a man as its leader

"Let him who has understanding calculate the number of the beast, for it is the number of a man" (Revelation 13:18). Revelation refers to a man who represents this antichrist power. Daniel 7 describes the little-horn power, which is a parallel prophecy about the antichrist: "I was considering the horns, and there was another horn, a little one, coming up among them, before whom three of the first horns were plucked out by the roots. And there, in this horn, were eyes like the eyes of a man, and a mouth speaking pompous words" (Daniel 7:8). This beast power has a single man who serves as its representative and leader. We will soon reveal who this is.

10. The man has the number 666

"Here is wisdom. Let him who has understanding calculate the number of the beast, for it is the number of a man: His number is 666" (Revelation 13:18). Notice that 666 is not the mark of the beast, but rather it is the number of a man. The mysterious number identifies the leader of the antichrist power. So who is this antichrist power? Some of you may have identified it already based on these ten characteristics.

There is only one organization in human history that matches all ten of these characteristics with perfect accuracy. The antichrist is none other than the papacy—the Roman Catholic church-and-state union. We will see shortly how this institution perfectly fits each of these ten characteristics. But let us be clear: there are sincere, loving Christians in the Catholic Church who are doing their best with what they know. This biblical antichrist warning is not about the people in the Catholic Church, but it is about a false system that has set itself against God. Once again, God gives this solemn warning for our well-being and safety.

Make sure that you carefully consider each of the following ten proofs to see how the papacy

perfectly matches these biblical descriptions in a way that no other power can. But first we must realize that this teaching of the Catholic church-state union as the antichrist is not new. The majority of Christian churches today started out believing and teaching this. In fact, the leaders of the Protestant Reformation taught this very truth.

Consider the words of Martin Luther, the best-known of the reformers and the founder of the Lutheran Church, when he wrote about the corruption of the Church of Rome: "We are of the conviction that the papacy is the seat of the true and real Antichrist."[1]

John Calvin, another prominent reformer and theologian, agreed with Luther on this issue: "Some persons think us too severe and censorious, when we call the Roman pontiff, Antichrist. . . . I shall briefly show that [Paul's words in 2 Thessalonians 2] are not capable of any other interpretation than that which applies them to the Papacy."[2]

The famous Baptist pastor Charles Spurgeon, possibly the most renowned preacher and theologian in modern Christianity, proclaimed in his sermon on October 21, 1866: "It is the bounden duty of every Christian to pray against Antichrist, and as to what Antichrist is no sane man ought to raise a question. If it be not the Popery in the Church of Rome and in the Church of England, there is nothing in the world that can be called by that name."[3]

The word *protestant* has at its root the word *protest*. The Reformation was a protest against the abuses and false teachings of the Catholic Church. Most Protestant churches today, sadly, have forgotten what they are protesting against. It is no longer politically correct to teach this biblical truth about the antichrist.

But at Hope Through Prophecy, through both video and print formats, we are committed to sharing the truth, no matter how uncomfortable it may be. We want you to avoid deception and be prepared for Jesus' soon return. We will now reveal the ten proofs of the antichrist!

PROOF 1   THE PAPACY ROSE OUT OF A WELL-POPULATED AREA

The Bible prophesied that the antichrist power would arise out of the sea, which we learned represents "peoples, multitudes, nations, and tongues" (Revelation 17:15). The papacy fulfills this point perfectly, as it arose in western Europe—the center of world civilization at that time.

PROOF 2   THE PAPACY RECEIVED ITS THRONE, POWER, AND AUTHORITY FROM ROME

As we examine history, there is no doubt that pagan Rome transferred its power, its throne, and even its capital city directly to papal Rome—the Catholic Church state. The capital of the empire was transferred from Rome to Constantinople, allowing the papacy to be the chief power in western Europe. History tells us that "the Roman church . . . pushed itself into the place of the Roman World-Empire, of which it is the actual continuation. . . . The Pope, who calls himself 'King' and 'Pontifex Maximus,' is Caesar's successor."[4] Clearly, the Catholic Church matches this second characteristic.

PROOF 3   THE PAPACY IS A GLOBAL POWER

No one would argue that the Catholic Church now has worldwide influence. Leaders of the most powerful nations in the world flock to pay homage to the pope. The power and influence the papacy had during the Middle Ages and has now in the present is undeniable. In fact, the very word *Catholic* means "universal." There's no doubt that the third proof applies to the Catholic Church.

PROOF 4 THE PAPACY CLAIMS TO BE GOD ON EARTH AND TO FORGIVE SINS

As we have learned, the Bible refers to blasphemy as claiming to be God and claiming the power to forgive sins. The papacy matches this fourth proof perfectly. Please brace yourselves, friends, as we consider this quote taken directly from the Catholic catechism:

> Does the Priest truly forgive the sins, or does he only declare that they are remitted? The Priest does really and truly forgive the sins in virtue of the power given to him by Christ.[5]

The entire Catholic confessional system is a man-made counterfeit to God's plan of salvation. Only God can forgive sins. Not only does the papacy claim to forgive sins but it also claims that the pope is equal to God Himself.

In 1903, Pope Leo XIII stated, "But the supreme teacher in the Church is the Roman Pontiff. Union of minds, therefore, requires . . . complete submission and obedience of will to the Church and to the Roman Pontiff, as to God Himself."[6] Consider this shocking quote by the same pope: "We [popes] hold upon this earth the place of God Almighty."[7] Friends, these statements are nothing short of blasphemy.

PROOF 5 THE PAPACY REIGNED FOR EXACTLY 1,260 YEARS

We have seen that a day in Bible prophecy is equivalent to a year. It was prophesied that the antichrist would reign for forty-two prophetic months, equating to 1,260 literal years. Let us see if this was the case.

Papal Rome received full supremacy in Europe in AD 538. On this date, there no was longer opposition to Emperor Justinian's decree that gave the pope control and power.

The papacy enjoyed absolute power over the nations of Europe throughout the Dark Ages, when the people were kept in spiritual and intellectual darkness.

Then in the year 1798, the papacy received what came to be known as a deadly wound when the pope was taken captive by the French general Berthier. This event marked the end of the papacy's dominance in Europe.

How many years passed between AD 538 and AD 1798? Do the math—exactly 1,260 years, a perfect fulfillment of prophecy! Yes, this is yet another specific proof that the papacy is the antichrist, a title that no one else can claim.

PROOF 6 THE PAPACY RECEIVED A DEADLY WOUND THAT IS NOW HEALED

When the papacy received this deadly wound in 1798, Napoleon's general Berthier took the pope captive, showing the vulnerability and weakness of the papacy, effectively ending its 1,260-year reign.

However, the Bible prophesied that this deadly wound would someday be healed. No one will argue the universal power, influence, and prestige that the papacy now has. In fact, the ecumenical movement's goal is to unite all Christian faiths together and end the protest that once helped define the Protestant faith. Bishop Tony Palmer, who was invited by prominent televangelist Kenneth Copeland to speak at an ecumenical assembly of church leaders, said the following after the event: "The real gift of communion is finding our brother. For those of us who have ears to hear, let us hear, because this is both profound and revolutionary. Pope Francis is calling us into an authentic communion based on the fact that we are brothers and sisters in Christ, not communion through our common traditions. This is a new way forward."[8] Palmer also boldy stated, "Luther's protest is over. . . . If the protest is over, how can there be a Protestant church?"[9]

Friend, a movement is underway to undermine the Protestant faith and reunite with Rome. The pope himself spoke, via video, at this same event: " 'Let's give each other a spiritual embrace and let God complete the work that He has begun,' he said, adding that 'the miracle of unity has begun.' "[10]

The pope's appeal for unity and his request for prayer was embraced by Kenneth Copeland, who erupted into " 'Oh, Glory! Glory! Glory!' and then said, 'Come on, the man asked us to pray for him.' "[11] He subsequently prayed for the pope, "saying that he too wanted the 'unity in the body of Christ' that Francis was asking for."[12]

The Vatican is at the center of pushing for this one-world religion, and Protestants are beginning to embrace it. But, friend, do not fall for it. The Bible reveals that this unity will lead to widespread deception—and eventually the mark of the beast. Unity is a good thing—but never at the expense of truth.

This unity with Rome would have been unheard of by the Founding Fathers of America. The United States was built on the principle of religious liberty. It was to be a nation without a king, with a church without a pope. Many came to America to escape the persecution of the papacy. But the Bible reveals that the deadly wound would be healed, and prophecy is being fulfilled before our very eyes.

PROOF 7 — THE PAPACY RECEIVES WORSHIP

A beast in Bible prophecy represents a nation. However, this beast of Revelation 13, the antichrist, would be unique in that it would be both a nation and a religious power that receives worship. There's no doubt that the papacy matches this proof as well. We all know that the papacy is a religious power, but did you know that Vatican City, the headquarters of the papacy, is actually a nation? In fact, the Vatican is the world's smallest country, taking up about 0.2 square miles inside of Rome, Italy. That is just one-eighth of the size of Central Park in New York City. Despite its minuscule size, the Vatican is one of the most powerful nations in the world and receives worship from across the globe, with more than one billion followers.

PROOF 8 — THE PAPACY HAS PERSECUTED GOD'S PEOPLE

The Bible prophesied that this antichrist power would shed the blood of God's people, the saints. The fact that the papacy matches this statement better than any organization in history simply cannot be denied. "That the Church of Rome has shed more innocent blood than any other institution that has ever existed among mankind, will be questioned by no Protestant who has a competent knowledge of history."[13]

Historians estimate that more than fifty million lives were destroyed by the papacy during the Dark Ages over matters of religion.[14] To his credit, Pope John Paul II admitted to and apologized for these mass murders[15], but his apology cannot undo these horrible atrocities.

John Wesley, founder of the Methodist church, boldly stated, referring to the papacy, "He is in an emphatical sense, the man of sin, as he increases all manner of sin above measure. And he is, too, properly styled the son of perdition, as he has caused the death of numberless multitudes, both of his opposers and followers. . . . He it is . . . that exalteth himself above all that is called God, or that is worshipped, . . . claiming the highest power, the highest honour. . . . Claiming the prerogatives which belong to God alone."[16] Considering the intense involvement of the papacy with God's people over the years, it would be shocking if its existence were *not* prophesied in the Bible.

PROOF 9 — THE PAPACY HAS A MAN AS ITS LEADER

The Roman Catholic Church state fulfills proof 9 as well. The pope is widely known as the visible head of this worldwide power.

Roger Williams, the founder of the first Baptist church in America, says this about the pope:

> The pretended Vicar of Christ on Earth, who sits as God over the Temple of God, exalting himselfe not only above all that is called God, but over the soules and consciences of all his vassals, yea over the Spirit of Christ, over the holy Scriptures, yea and God himself . . .
>
> Speaking blasphemies against the God of Heaven, thinking to change times and Lawes: but he is the sonne of perdition 2 Thes. 2.[17]

PROOF 10 — THE PAPACY IS LINKED TO THE NUMBER 666

The number 666 has been the source of great fear and intrigue for many, but there is no need to doubt the meaning of this number. Many have mistakenly believed it to be the mark of the beast, but the Bible says: "Here is wisdom. Let him who has understanding calculate the number of the beast, for it is the number of a man: His number is 666" (Revelation 13:18).

So 666 is the number of the beast and of a specific man in that organization. Who could this man be? Could it be the pope, the recognized leader of the papacy?

One of the names often given to the pope is Vicarius Filii Dei, which is Latin for "Vicar of the Son of God," or substitute for the Son of God. We have already seen that this is a position that the papacy claims. Notice what happens when we add up the Roman numeral values for this name:

Vicarius Filii Dei

V	5
I	1
C	100
A	0 (not used as a numeral)
R	0 (not used as a numeral)
I	1
U	5 (formerly the same as V)
S	0 (not used as a numeral)
F	0 (not used as a numeral)
I	1
L	50
I	1
I	1
D	500
E	0 (not used as a numeral)
I	1

Total = 666

These numbers add up to exactly, you guessed it, 666—the number of the beast and the number of a man, just as the Bible has prophesied.

Friends, God wants us to have no doubts about the identity of this beast power. In this chapter we have seen ten distinct proofs, all perfectly fulfilled by the papacy.

And this knowledge is essential, because it will be this antichrist beast power who will inflict the infamous mark of the beast throughout all the world. This will be the topic of the next chapter in this book. Friend, whatever happens, do not stop reading—your eternal life is at stake.

Once again, this warning about the antichrist is not an attack on our precious friends in the Catholic Church but against Satan himself and a counterfeit system of worship that positions itself against God. It is a message of warning and love from Jesus Himself, who wants all of us, including Catholics, to be saved in His kingdom.

If you are grateful for this powerful admonition from Jesus, thank the Lord for this message of caution and love.

The video for this chapter is on YouTube. Search for "The Antichrist: 10 Proofs From the Bible (It Exists Today)," or scan this QR code.

---

1. Martin Luther, *Schriften*, vol. 15, col. 1639, quoted in LeRoy Froom, *The Prophetic Faith of Our Fathers*, vol. 2 (Washington, DC: Review and Herald®, 1948), 256.

2. John Calvin, *Institutes of the Christian Religion*, trans. John Allen, 6th ed., vol. 2 (Philadelphia: Presbyterian Board of Publication and Sabbath-School Work, 1911), 335.

3. Charles Haddon Spurgeon, "Pray for Jesus," The Spurgeon Center for Biblical Preaching at Midwestern Seminary, accessed March 15, 2022, https://www.spurgeon.org/resource-library/sermons/pray-for-jesus.

4. Adolf Harnack, *What Is Christianity?*, trans. Thomas Bailey Saunders, 2nd ed. (New York: Putnam, 1908), 270.

5. Joseph Deharbe, *A Complete Catechism of the Catholic Religion*, trans. John Fander, ed. James J. Fox and Thomas McMillan, 6th ed. (New York: Schwartz, Kirwin, and Fauss, 1912), 279.

6. Pope Leo XIII, "Sapientiae Christianae," in *The Great Encyclical Letters of Pope Leo XIII* (New York: Benziger Brothers, 1903), 193.

7. Pope Leo XIII, "Praeclara Gratulationis Publicae," in *Great Encyclical Letters*, 304.

8. Tony Palmer, "Bishop Tony Palmer and Pope Francis—The Miracle of Unity Has Begun," YouTube video, February 28, 2014, https://www.youtube.com/watch?v=NHbEWw7l_Ek.

9. Will Graham, "Is the Reformation Over?" Evangelical Focus, June 19, 2016, https://evangelicalfocus.com/fresh-breeze/1703/is-the-reformation-over-tony-palmer.

10. " 'We Are Brothers,' Pope Stresses in Message to Pentecostals," Catholic News Agency, February 25, 2014, https://www.catholicnewsagency.com/news/29099/we-are-brothers-pope-stresses-in-message-to-pentecostals.

11. Clifford R. Goldstein, "Speaking as a Brother," *Liberty*, November/December 2014, https://www.libertymagazine.org/article/speaking-as-a-brother.

12. Goldstein, "Speaking as a Brother."

13. W. E. H. Lecky, *History of the Rise and Influence of the Spirit of Rationalism in Europe*, vol. 2 (London: Longmans, Green, and Co., 1897), 52.

14. Walter M. Montaño, *Behind the Purple Curtain* (Los Angeles: Cowman Publications, 1950), 113.

15. Rory Carroll, "Pope Says Sorry for Sins of Church," *The Guardian*, March 13, 2000, https://www.theguardian.com/world/2000/mar/13/catholicism.religion

16. "Notes on St. Paul's Second Epistle to the Thessalonians," Section 2, Wesley's Notes, *Christian Classics Ethereal Library*, accessed March 16, 2022, https://ccel.org/ccel/wesley/notes/notes.i.xv.iii.html.

17. "A Letter . . . Roger Williams to Major Mason," June, 1670, in *Collections of the Massachusetts Historical Society, 1792–1801*, 1st series, vol. 1, 200.

Much of this chapter has been adapted with permission from Dakota Day. Dakota Day, "Antichrist Unmasked" YouTube video, September 15, 2018, https://www.youtube.com/watch?v=bwVBv39GBWs

The Mark of the Beast: Prophecy's Most Urgent Warning

Many Christians are confused on what this mysterious mark is.
This knowledge is essential, because whoever receives the mark will be
eternally destroyed, and God truly desires a far different destiny for us.

Here is the fundamental warning: "If anyone worships the beast and his image, and receives his mark on his forehead or on his hand, he himself shall also drink of the wine of the wrath of God" (Revelation 14:9, 10).

What is the meaning of these words? What is the mark of the beast? We will go straight to the Bible to reveal with 100 percent certainty what is meant by the mark of the beast and how you can avoid it.

Because we are discussing extremely solemn truths from God Himself, I would ask you to please pray before reading this chapter. Before we reveal the mark of the beast, we will first review the identity of the beast itself and also God's mark, or seal, for His people in the last days, for which the mark of the beast is the direct counterfeit.

First, let us travel back to courts of heaven, where this conflict between good and evil began.

The beginning of the controversy

Lucifer was created perfect and was recognized as the wisest and most beautiful of all the created beings. In fact, he held the exalted position of covering cherub; in other words, he was right next to God's throne in heaven (Ezekiel 28:16).

According to the description of the earthly sanctuary, which mirrors the heavenly one, God's ark of the covenant contains God's holy law of the Ten Commandments—the unchangeable transcript of His character, the eternal code of moral living for the entire universe (see 1 Kings 8:9; Hebrews 9:4).

Lucifer, like all of God's created beings, was given free will. Instead of using this free will to glorify and honor God, Lucifer chose to rebel and allowed his heart to be filled with pride. He coveted the very throne of God: "You were perfect in your ways from the day you were created, till iniquity was found in you" (Ezekiel 28:15).

Lucifer became the first to commit iniquity, or sin, which the Bible defines as breaking God's law (1 John 3:4).

He broke the very law of the Ten Commandments that he had been assigned to cover and exalt in heaven.

Because he refused to affirm his allegiance to God, Lucifer was eventually cast out of heaven, along with one-third of the angels who rebelled with him (Revelation 12:4).

Why didn't God destroy Lucifer then and there? If He had, then the universe would have obeyed God out of fear rather than love. There would be doubts about God's character and His law. God is allowing sin to run its course, so that all human beings can see the results of sin and decide for themselves which master they will serve.

Now the war between good and evil rages on, and this planet is the battleground.

Lucifer, now known as Satan, roams this earth, seeking to tempt human beings, the crown of God's creation, into rebelling against their Creator and His holy law.

The Bible warns us: "Be sober, be vigilant; because your adversary the devil walks about like a roaring lion, seeking whom he may devour" (1 Peter 5:8).

Satan, in the form of a serpent, tempted Adam and Eve, our first parents, into sin, bringing death, pain, and woe to this world (Genesis 3).

Jesus Christ, the Hero of humanity, came to Earth to pay the death penalty for our sin (Matthew 1:21), the broken law of God.

Jesus lived a perfect life and kept His Father's commandments. Yet he died for us, that we might live.

Christ's death on the cross

Jesus' sacrificial death on the cross proved two things about God:

1. It proved that God is righteous. His law of the Ten Commandments is eternal and can never be changed. Even Jesus had to pay the penalty for the broken law of God, since He took our sins on Himself.

2. It proved that God is love. He sent His own son to die that we might live (John 3:16).

Throughout history, Satan has worked through various nations and agencies to try to tempt, deceive, and destroy God's people. They included:

- **Ancient Egypt, with its teaching of spiritualism—that the soul lives on after death.**
- **Babylon, with its heathen practices and sorcery.**
- **The brutal Roman Empire, which tried to destroy Jesus when He was a child.**

And as we saw in chapter 5, Satan would even infiltrate the church itself, using the Roman Catholic church-and-state union to persecute and deceive God's people.

But during every period of history, God always has a people that stand for Him, even in the midst of the most ferocious attacks.

This great controversy between Christ and Satan has raged on the through the centuries, and it continues to this very day.

Whether we realize it or not, each of us is engaged in a war, a battle for our very souls.

We must make a decision, a choice, as to which master we will serve: Christ or Satan.

Throughout history, allegiance to God has always been evidenced by one thing: obedience.

"Now by this we know that we know Him, if we keep His commandments. He who says, 'I know Him,' and does not keep His commandments, is a liar, and the truth is not in him. But whoever keeps His word, truly the love of God is perfected in him" (1 John 2:3–5).

Our actions, our decisions, reveal to God and to the universe who we belong to.

The mark of the beast relates to worship

Therefore, the mark of the beast, the final test for humanity, will be an issue of worship, an issue of obedience. Whom will we serve?

Before we reveal this infamous mark, we must remember the identity of the beast itself, also known as the antichrist. As shown in the previous chapter, only one power in human history perfectly matches each element in the biblical description of the beast: The Roman Catholic church-and-state union—the papacy. Again, this is not an attack on the people within the Catholic Church but rather a warning against a false system of worship.

Only the papacy, led by the pope as its visible leader, fulfills all of these biblical descriptions of the antichrist beast with perfect detail.

However, there is another characteristic of the antichrist that we must discuss as we prepare to reveal the mark of the beast.

In Daniel's description of the antichrist, we read that it would "intend to change times and law" (Daniel 7:25). Is it true that the papacy, the beast of Revelation 13, would attempt to change God's time and laws?

Yes, it is. In its official catechism, the Catholic Church has changed the Ten Commandments. It has removed the second commandment, which forbids the worship of idols, and it has split the tenth commandment in two, so that there are still ten in total.

But what about the time mentioned in Daniel 7:25? Did the papacy attempt to change God's time in any way? Yes, it did. Once again, in its official teachings (or catechism), the Catholic Church has shortened the fourth commandment that discusses the Sabbath, the only commandment that deals with time, from ninety-four words to just eight.

What is more, the papacy has openly and blasphemously defied God and His law by claiming to change the Sabbath day from the seventh day of the week, as the Bible commands, to the first day of the week, also known as Sunday.

Please do not take my word for this. In its official writings, *The Convert's Catechism of Catholic Doctrine*, the papacy states:

Q. Which is the Sabbath day?
A. Saturday is the Sabbath day.
Q. Why do we observe Sunday instead of Saturday?
A. We observe Sunday instead of Saturday because the Catholic church, in the Council of Laodicea (A D. [*sic*] 336), transferred the solemnity from Saturday to Sunday.[1]

The Catholic Church even boldly claims to have the power to change God's holy law:"Had she not such power, she could not have done that in which all modern religionists agree with her; . . . she could not have substituted the observance of Sunday the first day of the week, for the observance of Saturday the seventh day, a change for which there is no Scriptural authority."[2]

Does any man or organization truly have the power to change God's law? Absolutely not! The Bible says:"You shall not add to the word which I command you, nor take from it, that you may keep the commandments of the LORD your God which I command you" (Deuteronomy 4:2).

A false teaching has crept into the Christian church that says obedience to God's commandments is no longer required. Friends, this is a deadly deception that is not supported by the Bible. On the contrary, God tells us, "Blessed are those who do His commandments, that they may have the right to the tree of life, and may enter through the gates into the city" (Revelation 22:14).

And we have already seen that obedience to God's laws is the sign that we belong to Him. That is why it makes sense that the antichrist beast would try to change God's law in order to deceive people into disobedience and separation from God. In fact, the seal of God has to do with allegiance and obedience to God's law: "Bind up the testimony, seal the law among my disciples" (Isaiah 8:16).

The seal of God

If you ask any banker, the best way to discover a counterfeit is to learn as much as possible about the genuine article. So before we reveal the mark of the beast, we will identify the seal of God. This is particularly helpful because the mark of the beast is a direct counterfeit of God's seal.

In ancient times, when a ruler sent out a decree, his authorized seal contained three elements: his name, title, and territory.

So what about the seal of God?

We have learned that is has to do with obedience to God's commandments. Do any of the commandments have all three elements of an official seal?

Yes, there is one! Consider the fourth commandment:"Remember the Sabbath day, to keep it holy. Six days you shall labor and do all your work, but the seventh day is the Sabbath of the

LORD your God. [This is God's name.] In it you shall do no work. . . . For in six days the LORD made [this reveals God's title as the Creator] the heavens and the earth, the sea, and all that is in them [His territory], and rested the seventh day" (Exodus 20:8–11).

So we can see that the Sabbath is the only one of God's commandments that contains all three elements of an official seal—God's name, title, and territory.

Speaking of God's Sabbath, the Bible adds: "Moreover I also gave them My Sabbaths, to be a sign between them and Me, that they might know that I am the Lord who sanctifies them" (Ezekiel 20:12). Later in this same chapter, we read: "Hallow My Sabbaths, and they will be a sign between Me and you, that you may know that I am the LORD your God" (verse 20). The Bible reveals that the words *seal*, *mark*, and *sign* can be used interchangeably (Genesis 17:11; Romans 4:11; Revelation 7:3; Ezekiel 9:4).

In the last days, the devil will have his mark, but the Sabbath is God's sign, or mark, that will ensure that His faithful people will be protected and receive eternal life.

Let's review what we have learned:

1. The mark of the beast will be come from the beast power, which we have identified as the papacy.

2. The mark of the beast will be centered on worship—specifically, obedience to God's commandments. Another reason we can be sure of this is because the verse directly after the mark of the beast warning in Revelation 14 declares: "Here is the patience of the saints; here are those who keep the commandments of God and the faith of Jesus" (Revelation 14:12). Yes, in contrast to those who worship the beast and take his mark are those that stay faithful to Jesus and obey His commandments.

3. The mark of the beast will be a substitute, or counterfeit, of the seal of God, which we have learned is the Sabbath.

It is now time, friend—the moment we have been waiting for. We have learned that the seal of God is the Sabbath, but what is it's counterfeit? What is the mark of the beast?

What is the mark of the beast?

If the seal of God is the Sabbath, what is the mark of the beast?

Let us allow the beast power itself, the papacy, to answer this question for us: "The Church is above the Bible; and this transference of Sabbath observance from Saturday to Sunday is proof positive of that fact."[3]

Speaking of this change of the Sabbath, "the Catholic Church claims that the change was her act. And the act is a mark of her ecclesiastical power and authority in religious matters."[4]

Sunday sacredness is the mark of the beast. The alleged change of the Sabbath is the sign, or mark, of the beast's supposed power and authority. Now let's be clear. Many sincere, loving Christians worship on Sunday or believe it to be a holy day. We are not judging anyone's heart. God holds us responsible only for what we know or had the chance to know. But when God reveals truth to us, we have a responsibility to follow it, and it will be for our blessing.

It's also important to note that no one has the mark of the beast right now. We will learn when this will take place in just a moment.

Friend, only one day in the week is sacred—and that is the seventh-day Sabbath, which extends from sunset Friday to sunset Saturday.

"For in six days the Lord made the heavens and the earth, the sea, and all that is in them, and rested the seventh day. Therefore the Lord blessed the Sabbath day and hallowed it" (Exodus 20:11).

Notice that God blessed *the* seventh day, not *a* seventh day, and He specifically blessed the day in which He ended His creation of this world. Only God can make a day holy, and we have no right to choose another day.

By substituting Sunday for Saturday, the papacy has created a direct counterfeit to the Sabbath. As prophesied in the Bible, the antichrist beast would seek "to change times and the law" (Daniel 7:25), and in so doing, claim to be above the Bible—and even above God Himself. But what does God say about teaching man-made beliefs instead of the Bible? "And in vain they worship Me, teaching as doctrines the commandments of men" (Matthew 15:9).

How does one receive the mark of the beast or the seal of God?

Speaking of the beast of Revelation 13, the papacy, the Bible says, "He causes all, both small and great, rich and poor, free and slave, to receive a mark on their right hand or on their foreheads" (Revelation 13:18).

We know that the book of Revelation is full of symbols. What does it mean to receive a mark in the forehead?

"For this is the covenant that I will make with the house of Israel after those days, says the Lord: I will put My laws in their mind and write them on their hearts" (Hebrews 8:10).

Notice that God promises to write His laws on our minds. And it is the frontal lobe, or the forehead, where we make our moral decisions. The Bible reveals that the forehead is symbolic of our decisions.

Speaking of the God's seal, the Sabbath, the fourth commandment declares: "Remember the Sabbath day, to keep it holy" (Exodus 20:8).

And where do we remember? In our minds.

Accepting the seal of God involves making a conscious decision to obey God's true Sabbath—worshiping Him as the Creator.

In contrast, the mark of the beast can be received on either the forehead or the hand. What does this mean?

Again, the forehead is where we make our moral decisions: "It shall be as a sign to you on your hand and as a memorial between your eyes, that the LORD's law may be in your mouth" (Exodus 13:9).

The mark will be received on the forehead when someone believes in the false Sabbath, Sunday, despite the biblical evidence that shows otherwise. In essence, these are those who have been deceived by false teaching.

What about the hand? The Bible reveals that the hand is a symbol of work or actions: "Whatever your hand finds to do, do it with your might" (Ecclesiastes 9:10).

The mark of the beast will be received on the hand by those who decide to follow the crowd and accept Sunday as holy in order to avoid persecution, and they may choose to work on God's Sabbath. This group is not deceived into believing the false Sabbath, but their actions will show submission to the authority of the beast.

So we can be certain that the mark of the beast is not a physical mark. Remember, the plan of salvation and the entire great controversy between good and evil has always been based on our free will—our decision to either accept or reject God and His requirements.

The power of choice

The greatest showdown between good and evil will be based on this same principle—the freedom of choice. To suggest otherwise is simply not biblical or even reasonable.

Think about it—if the mark of the beast were to be a physical or outward sign, such as a bar-code, tattoo, or other such thing, then sincere Christians who have made the decision to follow God and even die for their faith could be tricked into receiving the mark of the beast while they are unconscious or incapacitated, without even choosing to comply with it.

Throughout the book of Revelation, the key issue in the battle between good and evil is wor-ship and each person making a *decision* to follow either Christ or Satan. The mark of the beast will be based on our decision.

When will people receive the mark of the beast? The Bible says, "No one may buy or sell except one who has the mark or the name of the beast, or the number of his name" (Revelation 13:17).

This verse also reveals that there will be an economic boycott against those who refuse the mark. The mark will not be just a religious issue but a political one as well. The government will require Sunday to be accepted as a holy day.

Since the mark of the beast will not be a physical mark, how will the government be able to identify those who will not be able to buy or sell in the last days? The Bible doesn't reveal exactly *how* these laws will be enforced, but it could be that the bank accounts of those who re-fuse the mark will be frozen. While it is possible that technology or a universal currency may be factors during this final conflict, these items will *not* be the mark of the beast. We have already seen from the Bible that the mark is a symbol for our decisions or actions.

The mark will be received when the civil authorities enforce the acceptance of Sunday as a holy day. When people comply with these decrees, when they honor Sunday over God's Sabbath, they will place the authority of the papacy over the authority of God and will then receive the mark of the beast.

But could such a Sunday law really be enacted? The fact is, it already has.

There are currently what are known as blue laws on the books of twenty-eight of the fifty United States of America. "Blue laws are laws designed to restrict certain activities on Sundays (or other specific days) for religious reasons to observe a day of worship or rest. Blue laws also may ban shopping or ban the sale of specific items on Sundays."[5]

In the eighteenth and nineteenth centuries, people were often arrested, fined, and sometimes imprisoned for conducting business on Sunday. It was believed that these citizens were actually breaking the Sabbath.

As our culture has grown more secular over the years, many of these Sunday blue laws have been repealed, yet they still exist in several states. Sometimes, it is the sale of alcohol that is prohibited on Sunday. These blue laws are often defended because they are seen to have both a secular and religious benefit.

What is the problem with these Sunday laws? First of all, the Bible teaches that the seventh day of the week, the Sabbath, is holy, and not the first day of the week, Sunday.

Second, these Sunday laws are a dangerous combination of church and state. Throughout history, when religious matters have been legislated by the government, it has often led to mass bloodshed of God's people. God's government is based on freedom of choice, not force or pressure. That is why the United States of America was founded on the principles of civil and religious freedom, and the First Amendment protects our right to worship God as we choose.

These Sunday laws not only violate our constitution but they are also a foretaste of what is to come, according to Bible prophecy. When church and state unite to enforce Sunday worship, this will be an image to the beast. This means that goverments will reflect the way the papacy, the beast, has used political power and violence to enforce its doctrines in the past. There will be a death decree against God's people who refuse to accept this mark of the beast—the false day of worship: "He [the dragon] was granted power to give breath to the image of the beast, that the image of the beast should both speak and cause as many as would not worship the image of the beast to be killed" (Revelation 13:15).

Even as we speak, the movement to keep Sunday holy is gaining prominence around the globe. In one of his encyclicals, "Laudato Si'," Pope Francis engaged the world in a discussion on how we are treating our planet and what we can do to improve. Interestingly, the pope used this encyclical to promote a day of worship—not the Bible Sabbath, but the first day of the week, Sunday. The pope stated: "Sunday, like the Jewish Sabbath, is meant to be a day which heals our relationships with God, with ourselves, with others and with the world."[6]

Students of the Bible will see this as is one more step in the fulfillment of Bible prophecy. Climate change, moral decline, or a financial collapse could all be used as an excuse to enforce Sunday worship.

What is more, the leaders of Protestant churches, which were once strongly opposed to the false doctrines of the Catholic Church, are now extending their hands to unite with Rome. Consider the words of Bishop Tony Palmer in a message to evangelical Christians after he called for Protestant-Catholic unity at an event organized by evangelical leader Kenneth Copeland: "The real gift of communion is finding our brother. For those of us who have ears to hear, let us hear, because this is both profound and revolutionary. Pope Francis is calling us into an authentic communion based on the fact that we are brothers and sisters in Christ, not communion through our common traditions. This is a new way forward."[7]

The pope also expressed his desire for unity, via a prerecorded video, at the event organized by Copeland. Copeland, who invited Palmer to the event, went on to agree with the pope's quest for unity between Catholics and Protestants.[8]

This ecumenical movement is simply a fulfillment of prophecy, which speaks of the world following after this antichrist beast power, the papacy: "And all the world marveled and followed the beast" (Revelation 13:3).

The Catholic church-and-state union, one of the most influential powers in the world, is at the center of this ecumenical movement, which will create a one-world religion in the last days.

In order for the world churches to unite, there must be a compromise in doctrine. And Sunday worship, the mark of the papacy's authority, will be a foundational unifying factor.

Unity is a good thing, but never at the expense of truth.

For more information on how this mark of the beast will be enforced, please read the next chapter, and make sure to watch this video on the *Hope Through Prophecy* YouTube channel.

Obeying God rather than man

I realize that this Bible teaching may be new to some of you. I know it was for me as well. But friend, I appeal to you today to go by the Bible. And remember, if it is in the Bible, we want it; if it is not in the Bible, it is not for us.

Some of you may be thinking, "But my pastor does not teach this." Or perhaps your pastor says that keeping the Sabbath is not important. What does the Bible say about certain pastors or teachers?

My people are destroyed for lack of knowledge.
Because you have rejected knowledge,
I also will reject you from being priest for Me;
Because you have forgotten the law of your God,
I also will forget your children (Hosea 4:6).

Friends, the Bible condemns pastors who are willfully ignorant about God's law. Many church leaders will encourage their members to keep nine of the Ten Commandments, saying the Sabbath is no longer binding. But the Bible says: "For whoever shall keep the whole law, and yet stumble in one point, he is guilty of all" (James 2:10).

How does God feel about pastors who make no difference between common things and holy things, such the Sabbath? "Her priests have violated My law and profaned My holy things; they have not distinguished between the holy and unholy, nor have they made known the difference between the unclean and the clean; and they have hidden their eyes from My Sabbaths, so that I am profaned among them" (Ezekiel 22:26).

Almost all Protestant churches have openly admitted that there is no biblical support for keeping Sunday holy, but they still observe Sunday and neglect to teach the true Bible Sabbath. How should we respond? "We ought to obey God rather than men" (Acts 5:29).

While we cannot judge the hearts of church leaders, we must put God first and follow the light that He has revealed to us. When we know the truth, we are responsible to obey it: "To

him who knows to do good and does not do it, to him it is sin" (James 4:17).

In fact, the Catholic Church gives this startling challenge to Protestant churches, for which they have no biblical answer:

> You will tell me that Saturday was the *Jewish* Sabbath, but that the *Christian* Sabbath has been changed to Sunday. Changed! But by whom? Who has authority to change an express commandment of Almighty God? When God has spoken and said, Thou shalt keep holy the seventh day, who shall dare to say, Nay, thou mayest work and do all manner of worldly business on the seventh day; but thou shalt keep holy the first day in its stead? This is a most important question, which I know not how you can answer.
>
> You are a Protestant, and you profess to go by the Bible and the Bible only; and yet in so important a matter as the observance of one day in seven as a holy day, you go against the plain letter of the Bible, and put another day in the place of that day which the Bible has commanded. The command to keep holy the seventh day is one of the ten commandments; you believe that the other nine are still binding; who gave you authority to tamper with the fourth? If you are consistent with your own principles, if you really follow the Bible and the Bible only, you ought to be able to produce some portion of the New Testament in which this fourth commandment is expressly altered.[9]

Friends, an attack and a breach has been made in God's law. His holy day, the Sabbath, is being trampled on by the majority of the Christian world. The truth is not always popular. But just like in the days of Noah and of Daniel in Babylon, and just like with the few disciples who followed Christ, God has His true followers who will obey the truth that He reveals to them, even if it is new or different.

God is looking for people who will stand for Him in these last days. The Bible describes this faithful group: "Here is the patience of the saints; here are those who keep the commandments of God and the faith of Jesus" (Revelation 14:12).

And this great promise is given specifically to those who keep the fourth commandment, the observance of the Sabbath:

> If you turn away your foot from the Sabbath,
> From doing your pleasure on My holy day,
> And call the Sabbath a delight,
> The holy day of the LORD honorable,
> And shall honor Him, not doing your own ways,
> Nor finding your own pleasure,
> Nor speaking your own words,
> Then you shall delight yourself in the LORD;
> And I will cause you to ride on the high hills of the earth,
> And feed you with the heritage of Jacob your father.
> The mouth of the LORD has spoken (Isaiah 58:13, 14).

What a promise! I hope you will join me in honoring God's true Sabbath day and receiving

the peace and special blessing that comes with it.

In the final days of Earth's history, when a death decree is issued against God's commandment-keeping people, who choose to worship God according to His wishes, a loud voice will echo through the skies: "Do not harm the earth, the sea, or the trees till we have sealed the servants of our God on their foreheads" (Revelation 7:3).

Yes, those who keep the true Sabbath day and have surrendered their lives to Jesus, will be sealed and protected in the last days!

Like He did with Shadrach, Meshach, and Abed-Nego in Babylon's fiery furnace (Daniel 3), God will use this great trial to test and refine our character and prepare us for heaven. And like He did for these faithful Hebrews, He will be right by our side through the great trial and will deliver us!

But those who receive the dreaded mark of the beast will suffer the indescribable pain of missing out on eternal life. You can avoid this infinite loss. I believe God has brought you to this information for a reason—so that you can know the truth.

We are now faced with a choice: Will we obey man, or will we obey God? Will we follow the crowd, or will we follow the truth?

The issue of the mark of the beast is all about worship, and worship is directly related to obedience: "Do you not know that to whom you present yourselves slaves to obey, you are that one's slaves whom you obey, whether of sin leading to death, or of obedience leading to righteousness?" (Romans 6:16).

Who will have the authority over our lives—humans or God?

Friend, Jesus is appealing to you today: "If you love Me, keep My commandments" (John 14:15).

Will you accept His invitation?

If you love Jesus enough to keep His commandments, including the seventh-day Sabbath, I invite you to tell the Lord, "I choose the seal of God and reject the mark of the beast."

The video for this chapter is on YouTube. Search for "The Mark of the Beast (Bible Prophecy Movie)," or scan this QR code.

Praise God for those who have made this decision! Continue to pray for the strength to stay faithful, and God will provide it. And most important, keep your eyes on Jesus, the Author and Finisher of our faith.

1. Peter Geiermann, *The Convert's Catechism of Catholic Doctrine,* 12th ed. (St. Louis: B. Herder, 1937), 50.

2. Stephen Keenan, *A Doctrinal Catechism,* 3rd American ed. (New York: T. W. Strong, 1876), 174.

3. "Sabbath Observance," *Catholic Record,* September 1, 1923, 4, https://archive.org/details/catholic-record-full/page/n3/mode/2up.

4. C. F. Thomas, chancellor of Cardinal Gibbons, in answer to a letter regarding the change of the Sabbath, November 11, 1895. Sabbathtruth.com.

5. "Blue Laws by State 2022," World Population Review, accessed March 16, 2022, https://worldpopulationreview.com/state-rankings/blue-laws -by-state.

6. Pope Francis, "Laudato Si'," The Vatican, accessed March 16, 2022, https://www.vatican.va/content/dam/francesco/pdf/encyclicals /documents/papa-francesco_20150524_enciclica-laudato-si_en.pdf.

7. Tony Palmer, "Bishop Tony Palmer and Pope Francis—The Miracle of Unity Has Begun," YouTube video, February 28, 2014, https://www .youtube.com/watch?v=NHbEWw7l_Ek&t=3s.

8. Prove All Things, "Pope Francis Sends Video Message to Kenneth Copeland—Let's Unite," YouTube video, February 22, 2014, https://www .youtube.com/watch?v=uA4EPOfic5A.

9. Brotherhood of St. Vincent of Paul, "Why Don't You Keep Holy the Sabbath-Day?," in *The Clifton Tracts,* vol. 4 (New York: Edward Dunigan and Brother, 1856), 5, 6; emphasis in original.

The United States in Prophecy

The United States of America has been a beacon of light and hope for the world—the land of the free and home of the brave. Could it be that the most powerful and influential nation in the world would have a critical role in end-time events?

In this chapter, we will learn how the United States of America is clearly described in Bible prophecy—and the shocking role that this great nation will play in the final days. Please keep reading.

We will look into the book of Revelation to see how the United States is vividly described in Bible prophecy. Make sure you read to the end, where you will learn the startling future of this great nation and how you can avoid deception!

The apocalyptic book of Revelation, in chapter 13, identifies two key world powers in the end time. We will now review the identity of the first of these powers. It is represented by a dreadful, ferocious beast with seven heads. According to the Bible, what does a beast represent?

"Those great beasts, which are four, are four kings which arise out of the earth" (Daniel 7:17).

Then the prophet Daniel refers to the fourth beast in particular: "The fourth beast shall be a fourth kingdom on earth" (Daniel 7:23).

We can see that a beast represents a king or kingdom. And as we take a careful look at all of the identifying points of this fierce, seven-headed beast in Revelation 13:1–10, we can be 100 percent sure that it represents none other than the papacy, the Roman Catholic church-and-state union. This first beast is also known as the antichrist.

This may be startling news to some of you, but this has been the common teaching in Protestant Christianity for hundreds of years. And I want to be very clear again—this is not an attack on the people within the Catholic Church but against an unbiblical form of Christianity that has openly positioned itself against God and the Bible. There are many sincere, loving Catholics who are living up to all the truth that they know. But the Bible is very clear in its warning about this beast power. For clear Bible evidence proving the identity of the antichrist, please refer to chapter 5 of this book.

It is now time for the bombshell reveal of the second beast of Revelation.

"Then I saw another beast coming up out of the earth, and he had two horns like a lamb and spoke like a dragon" (Revelation 13:11).

Who could this mysterious power be? We know from Revelation 13:10 that this beast arises after the first beast goes into captivity: "He who leads into captivity shall go into captivity; he who kills with the sword must be killed with the sword."

So when does this occur? We know that the first beast (the institution of the papacy) is given authority for "forty-two months" (Revelation 13:5). We have learned that this time period would end in AD 1798, when the pope was taken captive by Napoleon's general Berthier (see chapter 5). And we can be sure from a simple study of history that the Catholic Church saw a great loss of power and influence around this time. So which nation began to gain worldwide recognition around 1798? The United States of America clearly meets this description. It declared independence from Britain in 1776, penned the Constitution in 1787, added the Bill of Rights in 1791, and was universally recognized as a formidable up-and-coming world power by 1798. In fact, only the United States of America can accurately match this Bible description of a preeminent new nation.

But what does the Bible mean when it says that this nation would come up out of the earth? Interestingly, the first beast arises out of the sea. What does the sea represent in Bible prophecy?

"Then he said to me, 'The waters which you saw, where the harlot sits, are peoples, multitudes, nations, and tongues' " (Revelation 17:15).

According to the Bible, in the context of prophecy, the sea represents a highly populated area.

Sure enough, the papacy, the first beast, arose in the center of Europe, a key center of civilization at that time.

In contrast, the second beast, the United States, would arise not from sea but out of the earth—in an area with low population—a perfect description of the United States when it first began.

The two horns of the second beast

The Bible also describes this lamblike beast as having two horns. What does this mean?

Horns also represent kingdoms or governments in Bible prophecy. The United States was a very unique nation when it first began—its government was founded on two basic principles: civil freedom and religious freedom. That is why this second beast is characterized as having two horns. The US was known to have a government without a king and a church without a pope. This unique combination of civil and religious freedom has allowed the United States to become the most powerful and influential nation in the world.

I am grateful to be an American and believe that God Himself was leading in the creation of the Constitution and the beautiful freedoms that it provides.

Speaking like a dragon

But I must be honest, that is not all the Bible says about the United States of America. The following information may be startling, or even shocking. But remember, if it is in the Bible, we want it. If it is not in the Bible, it is not for us. We go on to read the following about the second beast, the United States of America: "He . . . spoke like a dragon" (Revelation 13:11).

What does this mean, "Spoke like a dragon?" How could the United States speak like a dragon? We know that a dragon represents none other than Satan himself. Satan often uses force and intimidation to gain followers, which is the opposite of God, who gives us free will and never forces us. The verse shows us that the United States will transition from being a freedom-loving nation to a nation that uses force to impose its laws.

So what will this look like? How will the United States speak as a dragon? It will do this in four specific ways:

1. The United States of America will use force and authority, like the first beast. "And he exercises all the authority of the first beast" (Revelation 13:12).

Just like the first beast—papal Rome—the United States will use its power and authority to enforce its demands.

2. The United States of America will cause the world to worship the first beast, the papacy. "[The second beast] causes the earth and those who dwell in it to worship the first beast, whose deadly wound was healed" (Revelation 13:12).

Here we can see that the key issue, the final showdown on this planet, will be about worship. It will be a religious issue. Everyone will have to decide. Will they follow Christ, or will they follow the antichrist, which the Bible identifies as the papacy? Laws will be enacted to promote unity with the Catholic Church to form a one-world religion. True Christians will be called troublemakers and even unpatriotic for not compromising in their obedience to God.

While it may seem that such fulfillment of Bible prophecies are unlikely to happen, we can be 100 percent certain that God's Word never fails. All the Bible's past prophecies have been fulfilled with 100 percent accuracy, including the one about the rise of the papacy, the change of the Sabbath and Daniel 2, which foretold the rise and fall of four world kingdoms twenty-five hundred years in advance. Only God knows the future, and He tells us, "And now I have told you before it comes, that when it does come to pass, you may believe" (John 14:29).

3. The United States of America will make an image to the first beast, the papacy. "And he deceives . . . telling those who dwell on the earth to make an image to the beast who was wounded by the sword and lived" (Revelation 13:14).

How will America make this image to the beast? To understand what this image will be, we must first review the history of the first beast: The Catholic church-and-state union. During the Middle Ages, the Catholic Church joined forces with the political powers of Europe, eventually controlling them in order to enforce the church's religious laws. The United States will repeat this same practice; the fallen Protestant churches of America will unite with government to legislate worship. The church's unity with the government to achieve its goals will produce the image of the beast. The making of laws enforcing worship is not only contrary to the government of God, who gives us free will, but will also be a trampling of our precious United States Constitution, which promises freedom of religion, one of the pillars of this great nation.

4. The United States of America will enact a death decree. "He was granted power to give breath to the image of the beast, that the image of the beast should both speak and cause as many as would not worship the image of the beast to be killed" (Revelation 13:15).

The great power and influence of the United States will be utilized to give force to this religious law, which we will learn about in just a moment. The church will thereby substitute the convicting power of the Holy Spirit with the power of the policeman to enforce its form of worship, and eventually, the penalty for noncompliance will be death.

So what will this religious law be? What will people be required to do?

"He causes all, both small and great, rich and poor, free and slave, to receive a mark on their right hand or on their foreheads" (Revelation 13:16).

It will be the mark of the beast that will be enforced by this church-and-state union in the last days. Concerning this mark, God gives us the most urgent warning in all of human history: "If anyone worships the beast and his image, and receives his mark on his forehead or on his hand, he himself shall also drink of the wine of the wrath of God" (Revelation 14:9, 10).

What is the mark of the beast? This topic was covered thoroughly in the previous chapter. As a quick review, we know that this mark is a direct counterfeit of the seal of God, which the Bible describes as observing the Sabbath in honor of our Creator: "Hallow My Sabbaths, and they will be a sign between Me and you, that you may know that I am the LORD your God" (Ezekiel 20:20).

An attack against the fourth commandment

The Sabbath is the fourth of God's Ten Commandments, and it is the one commandment that identifies God as our Creator. It was instituted at Creation for all of humanity before the Jewish race existed: "Then God blessed the seventh day and sanctified it, because in it He rested from all His work which God had created and made" (Genesis 2:3).

The Bible also prophesiesd that the antichrist power, which we know is the Catholic church-and-state union, would attempt to change the Sabbath: "And shall intend to change times and law" (Daniel 7:25).

Once again, whether we receive the mark of the beast will be based on our decision.

Is it even possible that the United States, a country founded on the principle of separation of church and state, would enforce such a law? Friend, it has already happened in the past. The previous chapter discussed Sunday blue laws, which are laws that prohibit certain activities on Sunday. While many of these laws are not currently being enforced, they still exist in several states and show that our government has already set the precedent for creating laws to enforce religion.

Moreover, do the papacy and the United States really have the power and influence to create this end-time superpower alliance? There is no doubt. The papacy has risen to an exalted level of worldwide prestige and admiration. Presidents and dignitaries from across the globe flock to pay homage to the beast. The Bible prophecy of Revelation 13:3 is truly being fulfilled before our very eyes: "His deadly wound was healed. And all the world marveled and followed the beast."

A false unity

Pope Francis has made it clear how he feels about divisions in the church, and he has called for unity. According to an article in the *Catholic Herald*, the pope said that "it is unacceptable to consider 'divisions in the Church as something natural, inevitable,' because 'divisions wound Christ's body [and] impair the witness which we are called to give to him before the world.' "[1]

The problem is that the pope is promoting a false unity—one that is not based on truth but would require a compromise in obedience to God.

As far as the United States, no one will question its status as the dominant world super-power, fully capable of enforcing some type of martial law, especially if combined with the

influence of the papacy and fallen Protestant churches who unite with it.

How will this Sunday law come about, and how will it be enforced? While the Bible clearly reveals that this will happen, it does not provide us with the specific details. However, as we consider the rise in technology and the world events taking place, there are many possible scenarios.

Perhaps a worldwide pandemic, economic crash, terrorist attack, nuclear threats, or even an overall moral decline could trigger a law in our nation that would supposedly bring us back to God. A cashless system or some form of modern technology could easily be used to identify those who do not comply with the government's decrees. But once again, these items will not be the mark of the beast. Whether we receive the seal of God or the mark of the beast will be based on our decision to honor or reject God as our Creator and His true Sabbath day.

False miracles

How is it possible that Christians will fall for this last-day deception? The Bible reveals, "For false christs and false prophets will rise and show great signs and wonders to deceive, if possible, even the elect" (Matthew 24:24).

The devil will use great miracles to deceive even God's chosen people. Listen to how the Bible describes these miraculous signs: "He performs great signs, so that he even makes fire come down from heaven on the earth in the sight of men. And he deceives those who dwell on the earth by those signs which he was granted to do in the sight of the beast" (Revelation 13:13–14).

HOPE THROUGH PROPHECY

These miracles will be used as evidence to support the counterfeit revival and to pressure the world to observe a counterfeit day of worship. What other miracles will Satan use to deceive the masses? As part of this great controversy between good and evil, spiritual entities will do spectacular things.

"For they are spirits of demons, performing signs, which go out to the kings of the earth and of the whole world, to gather them to the battle of that great day of God Almighty" (Revelation 16:14). Demonic spirits will be working at a fever pitch at this time. Satan and his fallen angels even have the ability to appear as someone they are not! We know this because "Satan himself transforms himself into an angel of light" (2 Corinthians 11:14).

Demons pass for dead loved ones

One of the key deceptions that the devil will use in the last days is the teaching of spiritualism, which claims that the human soul continues to exist after death. Spiritualism is a lie from Satan and is not supported by Scripture. To learn the Bible truth about what happens when we die and to see how spiritualism has infiltrated the Christian church, please watch my video on this subject.[2] Right now, let's just say that Scripture is clear in teaching that the dead are not conscious in any sense:

> For the living know that they will die;
> But the dead know nothing,
> And they have no more reward,
> For the memory of them is forgotten.
> Also their love, their hatred, and their envy have now perished;
> Nevermore will they have a share
> In anything done under the sun (Ecclesiastes 9:5-6).

The Bible teaches that the dead are truly dead and that the righteous dead will be given eternal life when Jesus returns and resurrects them.

Here is what the Bible says about the order of events when Jesus returns:

> For this we say to you by the word of the Lord, that we who are alive and remain until the coming of the Lord will by no means precede those who are asleep. For the Lord Himself will descend from heaven with a shout, with the voice of an archangel, and with the trumpet of God. And the dead in Christ will rise first. Then we who are alive and remain shall be caught up together with them in the clouds to meet the Lord in the air. And thus we shall always be with the Lord (1 Thessalonians 4:15-18).

Those who believe that the soul lives on after death are vulnerable to the deceptions of familiar spirits, which are demons posing as those who have died. Satanic beings will appear as beloved family members and respected church leaders who have died. They will claim to have messages from God saying that God's commandment to keep the Sabbath holy is no longer binding and that we are to honor Sunday in its place.

A false christ

Finally, Satan will pull out all the stops in a last-ditch effort to deceive and destroy God's people. In his crowning act of deception, a demonic impostor will even appear as Jesus Himself. The Bible warns: "Then if anyone says to you, 'Look, here is the Christ!' or 'There!' do not believe it. For false christs and false prophets will rise and show great signs and wonders" (Matthew 24:23, 24).

So how can you and I avoid these great deceptions?

First of all, we must know our Bibles.

"To the law and to the testimony! If they do not speak according to this word, it is because there is no light in them" (Isaiah 8:20). This verse reveals that we must test everything by the Bible. If it's in the Bible, we want it. If it's not in the Bible, it's not for us.

God's people in the last days will know that Jesus will not set foot on the earth at His second coming, but He will meet us in the air. God's people in the last days will know that God's Ten Commandment law is eternal and can never be changed (see Matthew 5:18, 19).

Second, to be protected in the last days, we must be obedient to all of God's commandments, which includes the seventh-day Sabbath. A clear description of God's last-day people is given in Revelation 14:12: "Here is the patience of the saints; here are those who keep the commandments of God and the faith of Jesus."

Most importantly, to be protected in the last days, we must stay connected with Jesus, learning to love and trust Him more every day. Jesus told us, "I am the vine, you are the branches. He who abides in Me, and I in him, bears much fruit; for without Me you can do nothing" (John 15:5). As we pray, read our Bibles, obey, and share God's truth with others, we will strengthen our relationship with Christ, who is the only way to eternal life.

While Satan and his agents are working tirelessly to deceive the masses, God and His angels—an army of heavenly hosts—are tirelessly working to save as many precious souls as possible. They are uniting with God's people, giving their words unstoppable divine power as they proclaim God's last message of hope and warning to a dying world (Revelation 14:6–14).

We must choose a side

Empowered by God, the messages given by God's people will spread like wildfire across the globe: "And this gospel of the kingdom will be preached in all the world as a witness to all the nations, and then the end will come" (Matthew 24:14).

In the last days, every single person will know the truth, so that no one will have an excuse. The truth about God's plan of salvation and the significance of the Sabbath as a sign of reverence and commitment to Him will be revealed to the world, including loving, sincere Christians who were not previously aware of it. In fact, this is already happening today.

All of Satan's fury will be unleashed against God's commandment-keeping people. They will be seen as troublemakers and the cause of all the problems in the world. As we have learned, there will be an economic boycott followed by a death decree.

But then, in the grand climax of human history, Jesus Christ will return with all the angels of heaven, setting the sky ablaze with His glory—the wicked will be destroyed, and God's people will be delivered!

Friend, you can be part of the faithful. You can join Christ in the air and go with Him to heaven, where eternal life, joy, and bliss await you!

Each of us must decide. On which side will you stand? There's a powerful old quote that reads: "The greatest want of the world is the want of men—men who will not be bought or sold, men who in their inmost souls are true and honest, men who do not fear to call sin by its right name, men whose conscience is as true to duty as the needle to the pole, men who will stand for the right though the heavens fall."[3]

God is looking for men and women like these in the last days. In order to be prepared for the final conflict, we must let God build our character brick by brick and allow Jesus to remove anything from our life that doesn't please Him. We are promised precisely the strength to accomplish this: "But as many as received him, to them He gave right to become the sons of God, even to those who believe in His name" (John 1:12).

If it is your decision to take a stand for God, and with His help obey all of His commandments, no matter the cost, tell your Father in heaven: "Lord, I will stand for You."

I praise God for your choice to follow Him!

Dear friend, we are living in the closing scenes of Earth's history, and these final events will happen in rapid succession. I hope and pray that you will make the decision to take a stand for God and obey all of His commandments, no matter the cost. This is fully possible by God's

powerful grace when we surrender our will to Him. I want you to be ready to meet Jesus in the clouds. I want to stand next to you on heaven's sea of glass and talk about our great victory in Jesus! Stay faithful to the end, that you may receive the crown of life.

For a life-changing book that reveals even more about America in Bible prophecy, the mark of the beast, Satan's battle plans for the last days, and how you can be victorious, order *The Great Controversy* by visiting the site connected to this link: http://store.hopethroughprophecy.org /product/amazing-prophecies/.

I truly hope this book has been a blessing to you. If you would like to enroll in free Bible studies, email us at Bible@HopeThroughProphecy.org. And if you would like to find a church near you that teaches the messages contained in this book, please email Church@HopeThrough-Prophecy.org. We are ready and waiting to help you on your journey. Remember, friends—keep your eyes on Jesus, the Author and Finisher of our faith!

> The video for this chapter is on YouTube. Search for "The USA in Bible Prophecy (End-Time Warning)," or scan this QR code.

1. Cindy Wooden, "Christian Unity Will Grow Step by Step, Says Pope Francis," *Catholic Herald*, January 27, 2014, https://catholicherald.co.uk /christian-unity-will-grow-step-by-step-says-pope-francis/.

2. Hope Through Prophecy, "Five Facts About Death You're Not Being Told!," YouTube video, September 5, 2019, https://www.youtube.com /watch?v=b1x9dW3MdkY.

3. Ellen G. White, *Education* (Mountain View, CA: Pacific Press®, 1952), 57.